HOW TO BE DUTCH

HOW TO BE DUTCH

The QUIZ

By Gregory Scott Shapiro

XPAT Scriptum Publishers

Welcome to *How to Be Dutch, The Quiz*: the questions that SHOULD be on the Dutch citizenship exam. At least that's what I think as the American Netherlander, who's been here 20 years.

This book is a follow-up to *How to Be Orange: An Alternative Dutch Assimilation Course*. Because how can you have a citizenship course without an exam?

In *How to Be Orange*, you can find some of the questions from the actual online Dutch assimilation quiz, such as this one.

You are sitting with a colleague at a terrace. At the table next to you there are two men kissing and caressing each other. You are bothered by this. What do you do?
A – *You remain seated and act as if you are not offended*
B – *You tell the men that they should go sit somewhere else*
C – *You say loudly to your colleague what you think about homosexuality*

ANSWER = A

If you answered C, I suppose you can stop reading this book now. As for the other answers, I understand the idea behind them. But what gets me is the wording of the question: *You are bothered by this*. Personally, I wouldn't be 'bothered by this.' But – to answer the question correctly – I have to pretend to be someone who's bothered by this, who is pretending NOT to be bothered by this.

And – according to the wording – the men are not just kissing. They are 'kissing and caressing.' If any couple would put on such a Public Display of Affection, I know plenty of Dutch people who would have NO problem saying, 'Get a room! *DOE NORMAAL!*'

The online assimilation exam also gives examples of how some famous Dutch people have scored.

- ✔ Jacques d'Ancona (TV journalist) 4.7
- ✔ Howard Komproe (comedian) 4.6
- ✔ Victoria Koblenko (soap actress) 4.0
- ✔ None of them achieved a passing grade of 5.5.

One year, the Dutch Assimilation Test appeared on TV. The winners were Chinese food delivery guys.

So welcome to my self-made quiz. It can't be any worse than the official one. If you're looking for an official guide to the Netherlands, this is not it. If you're looking for some odd Dutch quirks – in snarky quiz form – then this book is for you.

Before we take the quiz, let's review the Dutch track record so far. It includes a lot of things that you may take for granted. In fact, wherever you are in the world, you can play a game I like to call: Look Around the Room and Point to What's Dutch.

From Dutch product names to Dutch artists to Dutch innovations, there's a lot that's hiding in plain sight:

The artwork hanging on your wall.
The long-life light bulb in your hall.

Household soap like Axe or Dove.
The band who sang 'Radar Love.'

The microscope, the pendulum clock.
The first publicly traded stock.

Carrots that are orange. Wow, who knew?
And WiFi. Yes, that's Dutch too.

Capitalism as we
know it today.
Marriage for couples
who are gay.

The first operational
submarine.
That awful Senseo
coffee machine.

The first-ever Fair
Trade coffee.
Cassette tapes,
CDs, LEDs.

Keeping New Orleans
safe from the sea.
The Voice, that annoying
show on TV.

Kuipers, the bald
guy up in space.
DJ Tiesto,
dropping bass.

Dairy cows of the
Holstein breed.
*Basic Instinct,
Robocop, Speed.*

Lady Melisandre on
Game of Thrones.
(And Daario, the
guy slipping Khalisi
the bone.)

Miffy the bunny, so
cute you could eat.
And even blackface
Zwarte Piet.

Philips,
Shell, KLM.
Unilever,
DSM.

WeTransfer,
Heineken.
Anne Frank and
Van Halen.

MC Escher,
Hieronymus Bosch.
Rembrandt,
Vincent van Gogh.

Erasmus, Spinoza,
René Descartes.
Barney, world
champion in Darts.

The word *Yankee*, the
word *cookie*.
And Johan Cruyff, RIP.

But – if you boast for giving
the world so much –
Then you've not yet learned
how to be Dutch.

Published by XPat Media, Van Boetzelaerlaan 153, 2581 AR, The Hague, the Netherlands
Tel.: +31(0)70 306 33 10 / +31(0)10 427 10 22 – E-mail: info@xpat.nl

COVER DESIGN Jan van Zomeren
INTERIOR DESIGN Bram Vandenberge
PHOTOGRAPHS Afuk, Alex Boogers, ASS man, Bad puff, BARF menu, Big Dick Rabbit,
Black Kids for Sale, Brain Wash, Choko, Cystiberry, Die Neger, Dik Kok, Dutch Detour NO,
Homoes, KKK, Kut jas, Manwood, Robbers, Tiny Kox, TITS, VD Water, Vondel Kids,
Woonshop Hardon, Worst Croissant
FINAL EDITING Stephanie Dijkstra
PRINTING DZS grafik
DISTRIBUTION www.scriptum.nl

ISBN 978 94 6319 015 2 | NUR 370

www.xpat.nl
www.howtobedutch.nl
www.gregshapiro.nl

This book is a work of non-fiction, based on the life, experiences and recollections of the
author. The author reserves the right to adapt or streamline details for the sake of privacy
or expediency. Quotes, events and details are not a reliable source of journalistic accuracy;
rather, they are subjective tools used to tell a story. The author has stated to the publisher that,
while certain details may have been changed, the essential details are based on true experience.
Portions of the text have appeared in stage shows at Boom Chicago Comedy Theater, as blog
pieces on Dutchnews.nl, and in The XPat Journal. The author extends his gratitude for the
help he received in developing the material.

CONTENTS

Introduction 12

1 Dutch Identity   15
2 Dutch Bikes   21
3 Dutch Housing   26
4 Dutch Stereotype: Sex   32
5 Dutch Office Culture   37
6 Dutch Stereotypes: Drugs   43
7 Dutch Fashion   49
8 Dutch Education   54
9 Dutch Holidays   60
10 Zwarte Piet   66
11 Dutch Standards   73
12 Dutch Cuisine   78
13 Dutch Group Behavior   83
14 Dutch Stereotype: Cheap   88
15 Dutch Language   94
16 Dutch Environment   99
17 Dutch Politics   105
18 Dutch Health Care   111
19 Dutch Bikes Part 2   119
20 Dutch Service   125

In Closing 131
The Author 132

INTRODUCTION

Congratulations! If you've completed your Dutch citizenship course, it's time now for the quiz. And if you've *never* taken a Dutch citizenship course, it's also time for the quiz. If you don't score well enough, yes you'll have to leave the country. But don't worry! The questions are so subjective that even most Dutch people don't get them right. They'll be leaving the country with you.

Note: *How to Be Orange* was an attempt to contain only the most poignant first-hand accounts and avoid generalization. *How to Be Dutch* is a blatant attempt to take personal experiences and generalize the hell out of them. Are these questions the textbook truth? No. Are they the most recognizable examples I could think of? Yes. And hopefully the silliest as well.

And bear in mind, this quiz was written by an American. As an American, my knowledge of any foreign culture is invariably limited. Perhaps it's that American, egocentric, chest-thumping chauvinism that allows me to compare everything to my own myopic vision of what a country should be. It's the same eager crassness that finds itself in a historic Dutch brown café and complains that the beers are too small. And maybe it's my total lack of inhibition that allows me to flaunt my own ignorance, while being so very loud in criticizing a foreign culture. Then again, maybe when I go back to the United States, I'll have to think twice. The personal freedoms are hit-and-miss. The vacation days are nowhere near as generous. And there's a lot more time spent in stuck in traffic than biking. Maybe it's not surprising I ended up staying over here.

FOR INEZ

CHAPTER 1

Dutch Identity

It can be difficult to understand the Dutch identity. Even Dutch people have a hard time figuring it out.

QUESTION 1

What is the name of this country?

A – Holland

B – Nederland

C – The Netherlands

ANSWER = ALL OF THE ABOVE

In Dutch, the name of the country is *Nederland*, and in English it's *the Netherlands*, but the official tourist website is holland.com. Their ad campaign is 'Holland, the Original Cool.' And the national airline's in-flight magazine is the *Holland Herald*. Oddly – of the 12 Dutch provinces – only two have *Holland* in the title. This may help explain the result of so many Dutch World Cup football teams. Yes, there are legions of orange-clad Dutch fans, but they yell 'Holland! Holland!' And when the ball goes to the guy from, say, Friesland, a part of him must think 'I'm not from Holland.' And he misses.

QUESTION 2

When Dutch people brag about their country, what examples do they use?

A – Dutch sports
B – Dutch water engineering
C – Dutch brands

ANSWER = NONE OF THE ABOVE

Trick question: Dutch people rarely brag about their country. More likely, a Dutch person will first offer insulting opinions about another country. Then – when the argument has inevitably started – they'll most often defend their nationality with Dutch brands and perhaps Dutch sports. (That's C&A, respectively.)

In fact, one Dutch brand is 'C&A,' which stands for Clemens and Augustus Brenninkmeijer. (The Brenninkmeijers are like the Walton family of the Netherlands.) (But not quite as much money in secret offshore accounts.)

In sports, the Dutch have many reasons to be proud. In the 2014 Winter Olympics, the Dutch speed skating team set a record. No one team had won more medals in any Olympics, ever. At one point, speed skating coach Jillert Anema was interviewed on US television. Instead of talking about his own accomplishments, he started by insulting American football. And then – when the interview turned into an argument – he ended up defending the Netherlands by listing successful Dutch brands: 'When we'd sell our companies to the world, we'd all be billionaires. When we'd sell Shell, Unilever, Aegon... man, you're broke!'

So yes, Dutch bragging does exist. You just have to insult them first.

Afuk
This is the Frisian language center,
where they give Afuk.

QUESTION 3
How many nationalities are represented in Nederland?

A – 179

B – 180

C – 181

ANSWER = A & C

The mayor of Amsterdam recently gave a speech, saying Amsterdam itself has more nationalities represented than any other city in the world. But he admitted that the exact number is unclear: one census reported 179 nationalities; another said 181. They may both be true. There must be one guy from, say, Burkina Faso, who's dating a woman from Guam – who lives in Utrecht. When he sleeps over at her place, it's 179. But when she sleeps in Amsterdam: 181.

QUESTION 4
Which of the following is NOT true?

A – Nederland is in the top ten happiest countries in the world

B – *Nederlanders* are the most energetic in Europe

C – *Nederlanders* are pessimistic and think they will be worse off than their parents

ANSWER = NONE OF THE ABOVE

They are all true, as reported by news headlines around the time of publication. Yes, Dutch people are happy and energetic, which they apparently achieve by complaining.

QUESTION 5

How many times does the Dutch national anthem reference other countries?

A – 1

B – 2

C – 3

ANSWER = C

The Dutch *volkslied Het Wilhelmus* starts: '*Wilhelmus van Nassouwe, ben ik van Duitsen bloed.*' Literally translated, that's 'I'm William, founder of your country, and by the way I'm German.' Yes, German. Where is Nassouwe? It's in Germany. Another quiz question: Are there any other countries that start their national anthem by name checking another country? (I'm serious. I don't know of any.)

Spain is the second country referenced. The final line of the song is: '*Den koning van Hispanje heb ik altijd geëerd*' or 'My allegiance has always been to the King of Spain.' How many times does *Het Wilhemus* mention the name of its own country? Zero. Now, that's not unheard of (witness the USA). But can you imagine America starting off its national anthem: 'O say can you see – our British history? And Canada's nice. And a shout out to Mexico.' No.

(Yes, there are more stanzas to the song. And yes, it's an inspirational story of the Dutch revolution that bears a lot of resemblance to the American Revolution. But no one teaches us that in America.)

Het Wilhelmus also includes the line '*Een Prins van Oranje*,' or 'A prince from Orange.' *Orange* is a city in France. Hence a total of three other countries are referenced. And not just any three countries. As you can read in any history book, these are all countries that have invaded and occupied the Netherlands. Hence, the question: 'What kind of self-hating country has this as a national anthem?'

This would be the American equivalent of starting the national anthem: 'O say can you see? Vietnam was a FAIL. And Iraq was a lie, but then no one went to jail. Everything we've done wrong, we have put it in this song. And no, we're not done, because the list is quite long…'

Nederland, you have a lovely country. Lovely culture. But you deserve a better national anthem.

CHAPTER 2

Dutch Bikes

In the city of Amsterdam the population is an estimated 780,000 people – and 800,000 bikes. In the rest of the Netherlands, the situation is roughly the same. We don't know how the bikes are repopulating, but clearly they've outnumbered the humans.

QUESTION 1

While biking, you see a group of tourists edging toward the bike path ahead of you. When should you ring your bell?

A – Ring as early and as often as possible

B – Dutch bikes don't have bells

C – Wait until you are almost on top of them

ANSWER = C

Ringing one's bell more often than necessary is for tourists. And while it's true many Dutch bikes don't have bells, most of them do. Even broken down, old bikes will have their bells replaced before, say, their brakes. The most Dutch answer is to wait until the last moment and ring your bell frantically, perhaps yelling '*klootzak.*'

Dutch cyclists are very optimistic. As the weather gets warmer and tourists start to arrive, the cyclists continue at full speed, believing nothing will impede their progress. And they will ring their bells as if genuinely surprised that newcomers don't know the distinction between sidewalk and bike path. By waiting until the last possible moment to ring, Dutch bikes maximize the element of surprise for the tourists, who will jump out of the way in terror and yell 'WTF!?'. This is a tradition for the Dutch as well as for tourists who need exercise. It's called the 'Tring-Tring WTF' Diet.

QUESTION 2

When parking your bike in a row of bikes, you knock over someone else's bike. What should you do?

A – Set the bike back upright

B – Leave the bike on the ground

C – Set the bike back upright and then knock over more bikes in the process

ANSWER = C

In the Netherlands, there are so many bikes it's hard to knock over just one. In Amsterdam, the city has been removing bike racks and replacing them with white borders on the pavement. This strategy is designed to make life easier – not for you, but for bike thieves and for the city's bike removal teams. Either way, there is a cull of bicycle overpopulation.

When parking your bike in an area without a rack, it is likely you will knock over a series of bikes, falling like dominoes. It is also likely there will be witnesses. The witnesses may well be tourists, who may well be high on something and laughing hysterically. This is understandable, since what you've done is frankly hysterical. You will be tempted to ask them for help,

Alex Boogers
Teased much?

which – given their sense of coordination – is unwise. Simply set your bike upright and as many other bikes as time will allow (according to one Dutch source 'maximum 2 minutes'). And remember – any bikes falling outside of the white square on the pavement will be removed by the city. Don't worry. This is a natural process, known as bike euthanasia.

QUESTION 3

When is it okay to judge people on the basis of color?

A – Never

B – When you're in the Netherlands

C – When you see a group of bikes of the same color

ANSWER = C

In the Netherlands, it is never okay to judge people on the basis of color, unless they're riding a group of matching-colored bicycles. Then you can be sure they are tourists on rental bikes, who are far more dangerous than when they're on foot. They're possibly high, and they probably don't know how to bike.

QUESTION 4

When biking in a roundabout, what hand signal do Dutch people give upon exiting?

A – None

B – Half-mast hand signal

C – Full hand signal for bikes, cars and trams to see

ANSWER = B

The common-sense answer would be C. But to be truly Dutch, it's B. This answer takes into account the rules of the Dutch driving exam, which is divided into 'Theory' and 'Practical.' In Theory, yes you're supposed signal when you turn, high enough so you won't get run over. In Practice, Dutch people signal, but not too overtly, as that would be uncool. The Dutch way to signal is to look as if you have a muscle disorder and can barely raise your arm.

QUESTION 5

The Netherlands is a country of bicycles. Biking etiquette is very important. You are on a bike path, and you come across someone biking the wrong way. It is someone you recognize. What is the most Dutch reaction?

A – Wave but do not stop

B – Wave, stop and talk on the sidewalk

C – Tease your friend for going the wrong way

ANSWER = NONE OF THE ABOVE

If you want to be truly Dutch, the correct answer is: Both of you stop in the middle of the bike path and chat for as long as possible while everyone else crashes into each other trying not to hit you.

CHAPTER 3

Dutch Housing

Compared to the United States, the Netherlands has a relatively small homeless problem. How they manage this feat is a mystery, because it can be very difficult to find housing. Very.

QUESTION 1

When you get the keys to your new Dutch housing, what can you expect?

A – Set of keys, with an extremely detailed explanation on how to use them

B – Set of keys, with no explanation at all

C – Set of keys, with an extra 4-sided 'Cross' key, just in case

ANSWER = A & C

When receiving keys to Dutch housing, you will likely be given an extremely detailed lecture on what NOT to do – so complex you'll be sure you've missed a detail or two. This will leave you confident only in the fact that you will end up locking yourself out of your own house somehow. And then there's the mysterious 4-sided 'Cross' key, which is also called the 'China' key. There's a lovely Dutch tradition of using ethnic terms to identify an object's origin (see *Jodenkoek*) – or just to randomly insult an entire race (see *Negerzoen*). The 4-sided China key exists to be so clunky that you take it off your keyring – which will inevitably trigger the one time out of 1,000 that your neighbor will use their China key and lock you out of your building.

QUESTION 2
What is the rationale behind Dutch staircases?
A – To celebrate Dutch nautical history
B – To be efficient with space
C – To punish humanity

ANSWER = B & C

Dutch staircases are notorious for being bizarrely steep, twisted and inhumane – in other words, 'normal.' Some older Dutch houses feature staircases that seem to have been literally ripped out of old ships. Obviously, when floor space is limited, it's necessary to be efficient with space. But even in newer, more spacious housing, Dutch building codes still require steepness and a maximum number of twists and turns. It's no wonder the Dutch word for staircase is *trap* – as in 'something you fall into.'

QUESTION 3
Which are acceptable structures for Dutch housing?
A – Squatted flat
B – Abandoned shipping containers
C – Abandoned office building
D – Abandoned boat

Dutch housing organizations are rewarded for their creativity with unclaimed structures, such as boats, offices and, yes, even stacks of shipping containers. But if you try to exercise this same creativity by squatting in an actual house, you will be treated like a terrorist.

QUESTION 4

What is the Dutch version of 'Full Bath?'

A – Bathtub that is full

B – An empty room with a showerhead

C – A full bathroom, with bathtub / shower, toilet and sink

ANSWER = B

In Dutch housing, there is rarely a bathtub. More likely there is a showerhead in one corner, with not even the pretense of a shower curtain. Rather, there may be a squeegee, with which Dutch people can engage in their favorite pastime of moving water where they want it to go. The toilet will be located in a separate room, where the aromas of defecation can be more acutely concentrated.

QUESTION 5

Why do Dutch toilets have a poop shelf?

A – So you can get to know your poop

B – To keep you humble

C – Don't be silly. That's not a thing

ANSWER = A

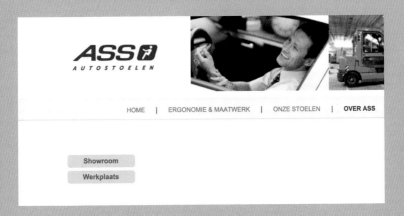

Showroom

Werkplaats

ASS
When you need automotive seating,
trust the ASS man.

Dutch culture is well known for treating sex as a natural part of life. Less well known is that there's a similar attitude toward the toilet.

The poop shelf was indeed designed as an inspection shelf, for making sure one's poop is 'on the level.' Whereas the rest of the world finds such a practice scatological and repulsive, the Dutch seem keen to pride themselves on what they've accomplished. When Freud invented the term anal-retentive, it is well possible he was referring to a Dutch patient.

Granted, the inspection shelf is not as common, these days. But Dutch manufacturers still do make the things. Recently, I went on a trip to a home improvement center, and there they were on display. I had to check if maybe they were old models that someone was trying to get rid of. But no, they were new. Clearly there's still a demand for the Dutch poop pedestal. There was even a toilet design named *Carice*. You may know Carice van Houten for her role as Lady Melisandre on *Game of Thrones*. Were the designers going for a pun on the word *Thrones*? Possibly. But I could only think of her *Game of Thrones* catchphrase, as it applies to the inspection shelf: 'The night is dark and full of terrors.'

In our current house we still have a toilet with an inspection shelf. Our house is like many old, Dutch houses built on sand: it leans over to one side. Thus, our toilet 'shelf' has become a toilet 'slope,' angled backward. Or – if you will – it's a like toilet 'stunt ramp.' Every time we flush, it's an adventure: will our brown heroes make it over the edge into freedom?

Americans have been accused of being loud and arrogant, as summed up in the phrase 'They think their shit don't stink.' But to our defense – at least it's submerged in water.

You want to apply for the Dutch *Stadsregister*, the Dutch housing registry. What should you bring?

A – Your passport

B – Your passport and work permit

C – Every form of documentation you've ever had and another 3 you never knew existed

The civil servants at the Dutch *Stadsregister* approach their jobs with a unique scrutiny. There is a chronic shortage of Dutch housing, because Dutch people treat housing like they treat their bikes: they get new ones without getting rid of the old ones first. As a result, you will need to provide many forms of documentation. The sheer amount of documentation is designed to convince you to move somewhere else. You will need passport, birth certificate, signatures from witnesses, and perhaps even an *apostille*.

The term *apostille* comes from the riddle 'Which follower of Jesus was actually French?' Only if you answer correctly, may you reside in the Netherlands.

Note: being registered at the *Stadsregister* is not the same as a *verblijfsvergunning* (residence permit). In other words, you may have permission to live here, but you do not have permission to stay.

CHAPTER 4

Dutch Stereotype: Sex

The Dutch treat sex as a natural part of life, which is healthy, really.

QUESTION 1

How can you best describe Dutch attitudes toward the Red Light District?

A – 'We don't go there'

B – 'Other countries have them too. What's so special about ours?'

C – 'We're proud of our adult-themed amusement park'

ANSWER = A & B

If you want to fit into most Dutch conversations, it's: 'We don't think about it. We don't talk about it. And if you do talk about it, you're probably a tourist.'

QUESTION 2

Which of the following is offered at a Dutch health and beauty shop?

A – My First Vibrator
B – Penis lollies
C – Candy G-String

In the Netherlands, you can pop in to buy some toothpaste and be confronted with the standard selection of a sex shop. Candy G-strings and edible undies can be found right next to the wide variety of lube and protection. And penis-shaped lollies have been known to pop up from time to time. White chocolate is somehow cheaper (which I assume is because it contains no real chocolate). And yes, Dutch health and beauty shops will offer vibrators. Specifically, the 'My First Vibrator' was a free gift with a subscription to *Viva* magazine. *Viva* features the 'Any Body' column, in which Dutch couples pose nude – with their heads cropped out. Are the Dutch exhibitionists? I don't know. But *Viva* never seems to have a shortage of nude volunteers.

QUESTION 3
What is the most disconcerting aspect for non-Dutch people in a Dutch sauna?
A – Female nudity
B – Male nudity
C – Their own nudity

When invited to a Dutch sauna most non-Dutch people will ask 'Do I need a swimsuit?' The answer is no. I once invited my brother to a Dutch sauna, and his first reaction was to bring his swimsuit 'just in case.' His second reaction was 'Oh, no! We're in the wrong changing room!' I had to explain that there's only one changing room for men and women. I watched as he had the same reaction I had, which was 'Wow, I'm living out in a 1980s teen comedy.' It was like wandering into a nudist camp. But the cheap thrill quickly wore off as he realized that many of the people getting undressed were couples. They get undressed. We get undressed. There's something comparatively appealing about the idea that this is all normal. And for any man accustomed to seeing female nudity online, it's nice to be reminded that most women do not, in fact, have breasts implants, and there is quite a bountiful variety. My first time in the Dutch sauna was with my boss. And she was really cool about it. She stripped off her clothes, looked me in the eyes and said, 'These are my tits. Yes, they're real. And now let's all relax.'

QUESTION 4
Which artistic inspirations are represented in a live sex show?
A – Figure skating
B – Ballet
C – Pornography

ANSWER = ALL OF THE ABOVE

Amsterdam in particular has a selection of live sex shows, which can fairly be called 'Bad Porn Live.' Especially for anyone sensitive about sexual content, these shows play an important role in desensitizing the entire process, reducing it to a joyless and purely

BARF menu
After the BARF menu, you'll want
to come back for more!

biological function. For those who are familiar with pornography, the live sex show makes the viewer appreciate how difficult it must be to perform pornography every night at 8, 10 and 11:30 pm. 'Imagine how much more efficient this would be if it was simply a video shoot,' the viewer will wonder. But – unlike video – the acts in the revue shows rotate, much like the stage, performing several times per night.

You may wonder, 'who signs up for this kind of performing?' Clearly these are pornographic actors who aren't satisfied with a simple video shoot. They will be announced like figure skaters: 'Let's hear it for Viktor and Irina!' Like figure skaters, they've chosen their own music and act out a number of poses involving legs in the air. And like a *pas de deux* in ballet, it is carefully choreographed. But unlike ballet, these guys go all the way.

QUESTION 5
What is the correct order for Dutch dating?
A – Date, sex, phone call
B – Sex, date, phone call
C – Date, phone call, sex

ANSWER = B

Many cultures advocate a getting-to-know phase before engaging in sex. Example: 'I've been dating someone for a few weeks. And I'm thinking it's time to invite him to bed.' Dutch friends of mine find this idea ridiculous: 'Why would you spend three weeks on a guy, if he might be crappy in bed?' In America, it's: 'Take me to dinner, then maybe you can take me to bed.' In Nederland, it's: 'Take me to bed, then maybe we can go to dinner.'

CHAPTER 5

Dutch Office Culture

Dutch meetings can seem like a paradox: how can they start out so much like American meetings, but end so differently?

QUESTION 1
When getting to know Dutch co-workers, what remarks can you expect to hear?

A – 'Nice outfit'

B – 'It's too bad American clothes are all so baggy. But of course that's because you are all so overweight'

C – A lengthy monologue on everything wrong with your country

ANSWER = B & C

Dutch people are known for being tolerant. But that doesn't mean they're not judgmental as hell. Dutch people pride themselves on being open and direct – sometimes at the expense of politeness, or tact, or respect for human dignity. When the traditional 'Dutch Honesty' is mixed with 'Dutch Courage' (alcohol), it can act like a truth serum mixed with Turrets Syndrome, causing involuntary spewing of every snap judgment, no matter how offensive.

Once I was performing a show at Boom Chicago comedy theater. Afterward, I experienced the familiar round of 'Hey, your nose is big! Are you Jewish?' 'And I overheard one drunk Dutchman telling my female colleague, 'You are the only woman wearing trousers. They don't fit you very well. Especially around the groin area. I told my friend it's probably because you have a full bush. But my friend says you probably shave. So which is it?' By the way, my female colleague was lesbian. I'm not sure when she officially came out, but that may have been the moment.

In America there's the phrase 'Never discuss politics in mixed company.' In the Netherlands, expect uninvited political commentary in the first two minutes of your conversation. Even right after September 11, it was not uncommon to hear, 'You know America had it coming, right? You funded the Saudis. You armed the Afghans. You could have known this would happen.'

Did it sting? Sure. But I must admit – in retrospect, the world would be better off if there had been more drunk Dutch guys in the Bush White House.

QUESTION 2

What is the best way to present your idea to a Dutch business meeting?

A – 'I have a great idea'

B – 'I like your idea, but my idea is better'

C – 'Your idea is stupid'

ANSWER = C

Option A is not advisable, as Dutch culture seems to be allergic to anything resembling '*opscheppen*' or bragging. That is when a built-in bullshit detector will kick in and cut you off at the knees. Option B is acceptable, but it goes against the Dutch belief in equality, and they may have to cut you down to size.

Saying 'Your idea is stupid' is the most uniquely Dutch response. As an experiment, you can try Option A 'I have a great idea' – and watch as the response is Option C: 'Your idea is stupid. The place you come from is stupid. And your beard looks like you have pubic hair on your face.'

QUESTION 3
How can you tell who's in charge of a Dutch meeting?
A – The one who's most dominant
B – The one with the most expensive suit
C – The one who arrives by bike

ANSWER = C

Most countries are rather hierarchical: the boss (who may well arrive by bike) says it; you do it. Not in Nederland. Like Dutch topography, Dutch management culture is flat as a *pannenkoek*. Remember when the Dutch were occupied by the Germans, the French, the Spanish? No? Well Dutch people do. Ever since they revolted against the Spanish Catholics in the 1500s, the Dutch don't like taking orders from anyone. This attitude still applies in many Dutch restaurants.

Big Dick Rabbit
I have no explanation for this.

QUESTION 4

Which quote best sums up Dutch meetings?

A – 'Since the Dutch are non-hierarchical, everyone gets to debate everything'

B – 'For most cultures, a decision is the end of the discussion. For the Dutch it's just the beginning'

C – 'I know what we agreed at the meeting, but I had some new thoughts about the meeting, so I think we should have another meeting about the meeting'

ANSWER = ALL OF THE ABOVE

European meetings sometimes end with 'let's agree to disagree.' Dutch meetings are more like 'let's DISAGREE to agree.' There's a phrase to describe Dutch meetings: '*Iedereen moet z'n plasje erover doen.*' Or: 'Everyone gets a chance to piss on your idea.' And if an idea can stand up to that treatment, they may take it seriously. However, this treatment can come as a shock for foreign colleagues. It's one thing for Brussels to have *Manneke Pis,* the peeing statue; it's another to act it out at every meeting.

QUESTION 5

Which phrase best describes the relationship of Dutch meetings to Brussels meetings?

A – Dutch meetings are short; Brussels meetings are long

B – Dutch meetings are from Mars; Brussels meetings are from Venus

C – Dutch meetings are *gezellig*; Brussels meetings are *blasé*

ANSWER = B

All summit meetings are a bit like sex. You have to seduce your negotiating partner. In that sense, Brussels meetings are more women-friendly: 'How was your journey? How are you feeling? Would you like some warm food? Perhaps some wine? A conference room? *Non!* No one's thinking about that right now. Have a *chocolat*. What's the rush? Tell me, what's on your mind? "Business," you say? *Oui, oui!* Let me take you to my conference room...'

On the other hand, Dutch meetings are like foreplay for men: 'Here's some coffee. Let's get to business! Business! Business! (cheese sandwich) Business! Ahh... That was good business. Want a cigarette? The smoking area is outside. *Doei!*'

CHAPTER 6

Dutch Stereo-types: Drugs

For many English-speakers around the world, the main source of information on Dutch drug culture comes from the movie *Pulp Fiction*.

I still remember watching *Pulp Fiction* in Amsterdam when I got here in 1994. There he was on the big screen: John Travolta talking about the 'Hash bars,' 'frites' with 'mayonnaise,' and 'a glass of beer in the movie theater.' And there I was with a glass of beer in the Kriterion movie theater… it was like he was talking to me!

But I watched that scene again recently, and I realized – since 1994 – a lot of details have changed. If Quentin Tarantino would remake *Pulp Fiction* today, the dialogue would have to be quite different.

QUESTION 1
Which of these lines is no longer accurate?
A – 'Tell me again about the hash bars'
B – 'What you wanna know?'

ANSWER = A

The Dutch term for 'hash bar' is 'coffeeshop,' which deliberately makes no sense. When Quentin Tarantino used the term 'coffeeshop' in his first draft, Americans were reportedly so confused he had to change it to 'hash bar.'

For the record, America also has confusing terminology – just not on purpose. For example, a 'drug store' is not where you go to buy drugs; it's a pharmacy where you go to buy medicine. In Amsterdam, you can watch American tourists ask for the 'drug store' – then watch as they are directed to the 'coffeeshop.'

QUESTION 2

Which of these lines is no longer accurate?

A – 'You can't just go into a restaurant and start puffing away…'

B – 'They want you to smoke it in your home…'

C – '…or certain designated places'

ANSWER = A & C

Since 2007, Dutch non-smoking laws include both restaurants and the 'certain designated places' known as coffeeshops. If *Pulp Fiction* were remade today, the dialogue might go like this:

Samuel L. Jackson 'So you go to a hash bar to smoke hash?'

John Travolta 'As long as you don't smoke it in the hash bar.'

Samuel L. Jackson 'Why can't you smoke hash in the hash bar?'

John Travolta 'It just has to have a smoking section.'

Samuel L. Jackson 'A smoking section?!'

John Travolta 'Yeah, you know. A specially constructed, hermetically sealed smoking section in the bar, to protect all the people who don't smoke.'

Black Kids for Sale
Where better to dress up in black face than
the shop called 'Black Kids for Sale?'

Samuel L. Jackson 'WHAT ARE YOU DOING IN A HASH BAR IF YOU DON'T SMOKE?'

John Travolta 'I don't f***ing know… !'

QUESTION 3
Which of these lines is no longer accurate?
A – 'Hash is legal there, right?'
B – 'Well, yeah it's legal, but it ain't 100% legal.'

ANSWER = BOTH

John Travolta 'Hash has never been legal, it's just that soft drugs are tolerated.'

Samuel L. Jackson 'Soft drugs – like mushrooms?'

John Travolta 'Not exactly… Since 2008, you can get some kinds of mushrooms, but not the good ones like dried mushrooms.'

Samuel L. Jackson 'What if I buy the mushrooms and dry them myself?'

John Travolta 'No one does that.'

Samuel L. Jackson 'Why not?'

John Travolta 'Because all you gotta do is ask for "truffles."'

QUESTION 4
Which of these lines is no longer accurate?
A – 'It's legal to carry it'
B – 'But that don't matter, because – get a load of this. If you get stopped by a cop in Amsterdam, it's illegal for them to search you'

John Travolta 'Since 2001, the cops can search you whenever
    they want.'
Samuel L. Jackson 'Damn!'
John Travolta 'And if they search you, you'd better have valid ID
    or you can be arrested. It's like back in Germany. You must
    have your papers, *und* your papers must be correct!'

QUESTION 5
Which of these lines is no longer accurate?
A – 'It breaks down like this: it's legal to buy it'
B – 'It's legal to own it'
C – 'And, if you're the proprietor of a hash bar, it's legal to sell it'

John Travolta 'Since 2012, it's only legal if your coffeeshop is
    beyond 250 meters of a school. And if your coffeeshop is not
    too close to the border with Belgium. And if you check the
    passports of all clientele to make sure there are no tourists.'
Samuel L. Jackson 'No tourists? Who exactly is smoking this
    hash?'
John Travolta 'Mostly tourists.'
Samuel L. Jackson 'Why would you keep the people out of the
    hash bar, who are the only people who want to go into the
    hash bar?'
John Travolta '… But it's still legal to buy it, it's legal to own it …'
Samuel L. Jackson 'Is it legal to grow it?
John Travolta 'No.'

Samuel L. Jackson 'Well, where does the hash come from then?!'

John Travolta 'I don't know! Hash fairies?'

Samuel L. Jackson 'But they're going to make hash legal, right?'

John Travolta 'Actually, hash is more legal in America than it is in Amsterdam now.'

Samuel L. Jackson 'I'm staying. That's all there is to it. I'm f***ing staying.'

CHAPTER 7

Dutch Fashion

If you encounter women wearing skirts over their jeans or men wearing orange trousers, it must the Netherlands. Men will also wear trousers the color of mustard or ketchup. This is to hide stains.

QUESTION 1

What kinds of undershirt are allowed for men?

A – Tight, white crewneck T-shirt

B – White V-neck T-shirt

C – A T-shirt showing Mr. Happy with an enormous penis

ANSWER = A

As for the Mr. Happy T-shirt, that will be worn onstage by a Dutch comedian, to be as distracting as possible.

V-neck T-shirts are apparently out of style in the Netherlands, based on the absolute lack of demand. While some cultures encourage men to loosen their collars and reveal a bit of flesh – or maybe chest hair – the Dutch are different. In a Dutch office, if men ever loosen their collars, it's to reveal the pristine curve of their white undershirt, as if to say 'Relax, ladies! No pheromones escaping here!'

Even the Mormons – who are required to wear special undergarments at all times – will take pains to hide their underwear from view when possible. But, like the Mormons, Dutch men obey the white T-shirt rule religiously, sending a clear message to rest of the world: I probably have tightie-whitie underpants as well. As they say online, 'A well-tailored suit is to a woman as lingerie is to a man.' If that's true, then the effect of a tight, white undershirt is less 'Victoria's Secret' and more like 'Victoria's full-length bathing costume.'

QUESTION 2

What constitutes normal dress?

A – Dressing as a huge orange lion

B – Dressing as an overtly racist stereotype

C – Dressing with at least one item of clothing from *Hema*

ANSWER = ALL OF THE ABOVE

If there are Dutch people with no *Hema* in their wardrobe, I haven't met them. As for the rest, normal dress is dictated by '*doe normaal*,' which depends on the calendar.

If it's King's Day, or if the Dutch national team is playing in an international tournament like the World Cup, then you may want to join in wearing orange – or go dressed as an orange lion.

As to racist stereotypes, yes there is a time of year for that. No, not *Sinterklaas*: Carnival. For Carnival, aka *Mardi Gras*, school children will feel left out if they do not come to school in costume. In the southern provinces, the adults will join in, and apparently the theme is 'No taste, no problem.' Many a Dutch party store will be happy to sell you an unabashedly racist costume, such as

Brain Wash
When you want to forget every
previous hairstyle.

'Chinaman,' 'African Hottentot,' and – for the culturally sensitive – 'Hip Hottentot' with blond afro instead of black.

QUESTION 3

A headscarf is:

A – A symbol of oppression
B – A symbol of liberation
C – None of your business

ANSWER = A

According to Dutch citizenship class, the headscarf is a symbol of oppression. Even if half the people in the class are wearing headscarves. Even if one of them raises her hand and says 'In Turkey, when I was growing up, a headscarf was not allowed. Now that I've moved to the Netherlands, my headscarf is a symbol of liberation.' The instructor said, 'If you want to pass the exam, the correct answer is "A headscarf is a symbol of oppression."'

QUESTION 4

Dutch women's hairstyles are frequently shorter than those of Dutch men. Why is this?

A – To look like men
B – To avoid spending money on excess hair products
C – To protest the monarchy

ANSWER = NONE OF THE ABOVE

It's so they can more easily grab their 'wet rag' (*watjes*) men by the hair and show them who wears the trousers in the house.

QUESTION 5

The Netherlands is the birthplace of the microscope and the telescope. What style of lens craft is the most fashionable for eyewear?

A – Large frames to highlight the large lenses

B – Ergonomically-tailored lenses

C – Tiny lenses that are hardly big enough to see through

ANSWER = C

The style of modern Dutch eyeglasses dictates that they should only call attention to themselves by being so small one wonders 'How can you see anything?' Perhaps that's why so many Dutch people bike to work: driving a car would simply be too dangerous. What most countries would call 'reading glasses,' the Dutch call 'too big.' The logic behind the fashion standard for Dutch eyewear is apparently 'It's such a tiny country, we wouldn't want to see too much of it at any one time.'

CHAPTER 8

Dutch Education

Dutch schools can be overachievers. They teach kids the things they need to know, as well as things they don't need to know, and even some things they probably shouldn't know. In terms of culture shock, Dutch schools can be 'a learning experience.'

QUESTION 1

Which of the following songs are you expected to sing when a child has a birthday at school?

A – 'Lang Zal Ze Leven'
B – 'Twee Violen en een Trommel en een Fluit'
C – 'Hanky Panky Shanghai'

ANSWER = ALL OF THE ABOVE AND MORE

When dropping off your young child at school, there may be a birthday in the class. If you don't leave before the singing begins, you can kiss the next half hour goodbye. Singing only one song is apparently a gesture of disrespect. Due to Birthday Song Escalation, there is a wide variety of melodies and lyrics from 'Long Shall You Live – in the Glory!' to 'Two Violins, a Drum and a Flute' to the wonderfully politically incorrect 'Hanky Panky

Shanghai.' This is a song, to the tune of 'Happy Birthday,' with choreography – namely, making slanty-eyed faces while singing about Shanghai. Of course if there are any Chinese children in the classroom, they will be invited to join in just like everyone else. It's equal-opportunity racism.

QUESTION 2

Which of the following lessons describes Dutch social-ization?

A – *'Doe normaal'*

B – *'Hoge bomen vangen veel wind'*

C – *'Steek je hoofd niet boven het maaiveld uit anders wordt 'ie afgehakt'*

ANSWER = ALL OF THE ABOVE

✔ *'Doe normaal'* translates to 'Just act normal.'

✔ *'Hoge bomen vangen veel wind'* is 'the tallest trees get the most wind.' The harder you try, the more resistance you get.

✔ *'Steek je hoofd niet boven het maaiveld uit anders wordt 'ie afgehakt.'* is 'Don't stick your neck out, or your head will get chopped off.'

While Dutch culture has a history of being tolerant, there's also a history of Calvinism that says 'Sit the f*** down.'

In America, children grow up with a different type of socialization. We hear phrases like 'Just do it' or 'Be the Best.' There's even 'The squeakiest wheel gets the oil.' In other words: 'To get the attention you deserve, it helps to be loud and obnoxious.' In Dutch schools, it's: 'Keep your head down, or get decapitated.'

It's like the time my daughter was accepted to train with a professional ballet company. My American family reacted with 'Amazing' and 'Awesome' and 'You go, girl!' The Dutch parents from her class reacted with 'Ooh, that sounds like a big change' and 'Will that be too heavy for her?' and even 'Are you sure you're not just forcing your dreams on her?' As it turns out, she did it and loved it. When parents from her old school would ask how she was doing I'd tell them the truth: 'She's doing great!' And they'd frown and shake their heads. So instead I started telling people 'It's heavy. Lots of work.' And they'd say 'Ooh! Tell me more!'

QUESTION 3
What is meant by the term 'black school'?
A – A school for non-white students
B – A school for which tuition is paid under the table
C – A school teaching students how to be black

ANSWER = A

A 'black school' is defined as 'a school with at least 60% students of non-Dutch origin.' The Netherlands has a reputation for tolerance and acceptance – so any students who aren't 'Dutch enough' are simply labeled 'black.' Note: Dutch schools do not practice segregation. As many Dutch parents put it, 'There are plenty of white kids in the "black" schools.' It's just that they don't seem to want their white kid to join them.

Choko
Chocolate milk so good
you'll choke.

QUESTION 4
At what age do Dutch children learn about slavery?

A – Primary school

B – Junior High school

C – High school

D – By accident

ANSWER = D

If Dutch children learn about the Dutch slave trade, it's largely by accident. Maybe it's because Dutch history books are modest and they don't like to brag. So they don't take too much credit for anything, even if it's something as notable as the Atlantic Slave Trade, history's largest forced intercontinental migration. Dutch history books are more comfortable covering slavery in terms of who *bought* the slaves, not who sold them.

Luckily, there's the Dutch national institute for Slavery, NiNsee, whose job is to provide education and awareness about this vital chapter in Dutch history. At least that was the case until 2011, when the Dutch government completely cut their funding. *Doei!*

QUESTION 5
At what age do Dutch kids grow up?

A – 11

B – 18

C – They never grow up

ANSWER = A

I was reading one of those articles about how Dutch kids are the happiest in the world. Every so often someone does a survey and finds that – instead of pushing kids to perform well on tests – Dutch schools lets kids be kids. It makes sense. What do you know? Kids are happier without homework! I've also noticed this trend with my own kids – up to a point. That point is called 11 years of age.

You know the American ritual called 'Going to College?' It's the biggest decision of your life up to that point, and it normally takes place at age 17. Dutch kids have to make that kind of decision around age 11. And it's not just about the school; it's about the *category* of school and the right trajectory for the career you want. Do you want to make things with your hands? Do you want to work in management? Do you want to focus on academia and research? 'You're 11, time to make up your mind and move on with your life!'

Yes, the Dutch school system lets kids be kids. Until it yanks them by the hair, smacks them in the face, and says 'Get a job!'

CHAPTER 9

Dutch Holidays

If you can make the effort to understand the logic behind Dutch holidays, then you will understand more than most Dutch people.

QUESTION 1

Which of the following is NOT a national holiday?

A – New Year's Day

B – Easter Monday

C – King's Day

D – Liberation Day

E – Ascension Day

F – Second Ascension Day

G – Pentecost

H – Second Pentecost

I – Boxing Day

ANSWER = F

Boxing Day is a holiday when you visit your in-laws and end up boxing with them because they apparently weren't good enough to spend the first Christmas Day with. New Year's Day is a holiday for practical reasons, mostly because everyone was out the night before, suffering fireworks-related injuries, and no one would come in to work anyway.

The rest of the holidays employ a logic that can be hard to follow. Easter Monday is a holiday because a majority of modern Dutch people describe themselves as 'non-religious.' King's Day is a holiday because it used to be the Queen's birthday. Ascension Day (*Hemelvaart*) and Pentecost (*Pinksteren*) are holidays because – though the Dutch are not actively religious – it's important for them to take not one, but two days off while they're at it.

BUT 2016 was an exception: there was no Second Ascension Day. Why? Perhaps because the Netherlands was hosting the EU Presidency, and it's a bit embarrassing if the whole country is closed for the *entire* month of May. If you want to be entertained, ask why the shops are closed on *Hemelvaart* and *Pinksteren* days, and watch as no two people give the same answer. The closest they come is because 'It's from the Bible... you know, the time Jesus took a 4-day weekend.'

QUESTION 2
Where do most Dutch people go for summer holidays?
A – Nederland
B – Southern Europe
C – Outside Europe

ANSWER = B

Summer in Nederland is like a flooding drill. Everyone pretends like the country is finally underwater, so they pack up everything they own and drive south. To go camping, do not buy a camper. Rather, drag a *sleurhut* – aka 'caravan' – along behind the car. Of course it is possible to be more economical. Some people prefer to simply squeeze everything they own into the back of their car, including peanut butter, potatoes, and Senseo coffee machine 'because they might not have coffee in France.'

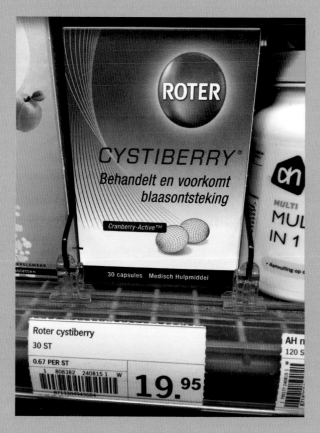

Cystiberry
'We need a name for a fruit-flavored pill to prevent bladder problems.' 'How about CYSTIBERRY?' 'Nailed it.'

QUESTION 3

Which is NOT a common way to celebrate King's Day?

A – Wearing orange and indulging in substance abuse

B – Wearing orange and selling a bunch of your old crap

C – Wearing orange and making your kids sing and dance for money

D – Not wearing orange and celebrating the Dutch Republic

ANSWER = D

On King's Day, the Dutch dress in orange to honor the royal House of Orange, which originated with Willem van Oranje in the 1500s. The so-called founding father of the Netherlands, Willem van Oranje, led the revolution to overthrow the Spanish monarchy in an effort to create a republic. To honor his wishes – instead of having an Independence Day from monarchy – the Dutch celebrate the birthday of the current monarch.

It is quite common to join the orange-clad crowd in the nearest city center and abuse the substance of your choice. Since King's Day is also the beginning of the official tourist season, be sure to tell any arriving tourists 'Yes, we do this every day.' But a truly Dutch way to celebrate is to set up a mini-stand and get rid of a bunch of old crap. Especially since it's a tiny country – and storage space in the average home is highly valued – the act of freeing up your closets and attic can feel a lot like Christmas.

If you have children and they don't want to part with their old crap, feel free to make them sing and dance for money. Warning: they may also rope you into creating elaborate games of skill involving cans and balls and lots of rope. One year I even encountered an entire performance piece called the 'Peep Show,' in which ten year-old girls were tempting passersby to insert their heads into a tent for 1 euro. Inside the tent was a group of toddlers, dressed as baby chickens, saying 'Peep! Peep! Peep!'

In the Netherlands, even the kids are politically incorrect.

QUESTION 4

On which occasion is it more important to give gifts to children?

A – 5th of December for *Sinterklaas*
B – 25th of December for Christmas
C – Both

ANSWER = A

Yes, *Sinterklaas* still wins. But Christmas is gaining in popularity. Some Dutch purists lament that *Sinterklaas* should be for toys, and Christmas should be for Jesus. Even though most 7-year-olds say 'How am I supposed to believe in Jesus if he doesn't bring me toys?'

QUESTION 5

Why do the Dutch light fireworks on New Year's Eve?

A – To chase evil spirits away
B – To make New Year's Eve extra festive
C – Because the Chinese did it and the Dutch took it over

ANSWER = B

After the countdown on New Year's Eve, the Netherlands has many more 'bombs bursting in air' than America on the 4th of

July. And most bombs are fired by individuals, as fireworks are legal in the days and hours leading up to the New Year. However, some officials are considering banning fireworks – apparently in order to support the Belgian black market.

Even when the Dutch economy is in recession, Dutch fireworks spending continues to break records every year. What better way to celebrate a crisis than to take your investments and literally watch them go up in smoke?

CHAPTER 10

Zwarte Piet

In the Netherlands, every November heralds the arrival of Sinterklaas with his white horse and his army of *negers*.

As Dutch people will explain, the word *neger* is not offensive, because it simply means 'black person.' And each member of the group is called *Zwarte Piet*. And as Dutch people will explain, Zwarte Piet is not offensive, because it's only white people dressed in blackface.

Dutch culture is famous for its pragmatic solutions to thorny social problems, but there seems to be a pretty big blind spot for Zwarte Piet. For example, when President Barack Obama visited the Netherlands, and Prime Minister Mark Rutte was asked about Zwarte Piet, Rutte responded: '…My friends in the Dutch Antilles, they are very happy when they have Sinterklaas because they don't have to paint their faces.' In essence: 'Welcome to the Netherlands! You black people look like you have soot on your face.'

QUESTION 1
Your young daughter sees a black person on the 5th of December. How should she react?

A – By respecting their privacy
B – By giving a friendly nod
C – By pointing and screaming, 'Zwarte Piet!'

ANSWER = A

Unfortunately, that is not always the case. At our home, we celebrate Sinterklaas on the 5th of December in what my wife calls the 'traditional Dutch way.' That is to say, we do it as cheaply as possible. We get a sack full of presents and we give it to the neighbor. The neighbor waits five minutes and drops the sack at our door, then rings the doorbell and runs away. The kids then open the door and – even though there's no one there – they scream and cheer 'Zwarte Piet!' It's the most cost-effective special effect ever.

One year, when my daughter was three, we finished dinner early and got ready for Zwarte Piet and gifts. It was almost 6 o'clock, it was already dark, and – before my wife could say 'Zwarte Piet will be here soon' – we heard the doorbell ring. My wife looked at me to ask, 'Did you go to the neighbor already?' I shook my head no. But my daughter – being three years old – was already at the door. She yelled 'Yay!' and whipped open the door. And there, standing in the doorway, was a guy with a black face, dark curly hair and a brightly colored red & yellow outfit. The outfit said 'DHL Post.'

Now I don't know whose decision it was to send this guy out delivering packages on the 5th of December. But sure enough, my daughter was living the dream, her eyes filled with joy. I was looking at her, thinking, 'Please, don't say it…' and I moved towards her, but not quickly enough. She raised her hand and yelled, 'Zwarte Piet!'

I stood there frozen, as the color drained from my face. My eyes locked with the DHL guy as I got whiter, and he got redder. The American in me was thinking, 'My daughter is a racist!' But the Dutch part of me was saying, 'That's right! It IS Zwarte Piet! Sometimes Papa has to sign Zwarte Piet's Magic Clipboard! And tonight Papa is going to give Zwarte Piet 5 euros.' And I shut the door as quickly as I could. I looked at my wife to ask 'What should I have done?' And she was mad at me. Her response: 'Why would you give away 5 euros?'

QUESTION 2
Which of the following did NOT appear on Twitter in relation to criticism of Zwarte Piet?

A – 'You're only here because you're black'

B – 'My ancestors indeed forced your ancestors onto the boats. Those were the days. Now your sort has too much freedom'

C – 'F** the f*** off if you think Zwarte Piet is racist… you're retards.'

D – 'F*** off you black monkeys. Next you'll want to close all the zoos because you're afraid you might meet an ancestor'

ANSWER = A

That quote was attributed to Dutch football legend Johan Cruyff, as he was talking to Edgar Davids during a board meeting for Amsterdam Ajax. But he could get away with it, because they thought he was Jesus. RIP.

Dik Kok
Gather 'round! The Dick Kok wagon's here!

QUESTION 3

Which of the following did NOT condemn the blackface tradition of Zwarte Piet?

A – UN Representative Verene Shepherd

B – UN Committee on the Elimination of Racial Discrimination

C – Rev. Jesse Jackson

ANSWER = C

In 2013, the UN's Verene Shepherd referred to the blackface tradition of Zwarte Piet as 'colonial.' She then suggested that the Netherlands drop the entire Sinterklaas tradition in favor of Christmas – which is technically her culture asserting dominance over another culture – which is by definition 'colonial.'

In 2010, US civil rights leader Jesse Jackson was asked if he thought blackface was racist. Jackson replied, 'I've looked into the hearts of Dutch people, and I have to take into consideration that they are some of the most tolerant, integrated, interracial people I've ever seen. And so – when Dutch people say they don't mean it to be racist – I believe they do not mean it to be racist… but the afro and the big lips have got to go.'

QUESTION 4

Which alternative Zwarte Piet character has NOT been tried?

A – Rainbow Piet

B – *Kaas* Piet (Cheese Piet)

C – *Stroopwafel* Piet (Sugar Cookie Piet)

D – Gold Piet

E – Soot & Beard Piet

Dutch people pride themselves on their common-sense, pragmatic approach to problem-solving. So, instead of actually making Zwarte Piet look like someone who came down a chimney, they try every other option imaginable. Rainbow Piet was laughed off the parade route in the 1990s. Cheese Pete looks like he has jaundice, and Sugar Cookie Piet looks like he has a flesh-eating virus. Soot-face Pete, or *Roete* Piet, is already being phased into Amsterdam's annual parade. Understandably, those dressing as Zwarte Piet are concerned that soot won't provide enough of a disguise for the little ones.

The idea of soot plus a beard – like Sinterklaas wears – has apparently not occurred to anyone.

QUESTION 5

Which cookies are currently sold in the Netherlands?

A – *Neger Zoenen*
B – *Choco Zoenen*
C – *Negen Zoete*

For years, Dutch confectioner Buys produced chocolate-covered marshmallow cookies called *Neger Zoenen*. (*Zoenen* means kisses.) (*Neger* you can guess.) At some point, an anti-discrimination group politely asked 'Would you be able to sell more of your product without pointlessly insulting an entire color of people?' And the answer was *Choco Zoenen*. But they are now simply called '*Zoenen*.' No shame, no blame. Just change the name.

The supermarket chain Albert Heijn now makes its own version of the cookie, which they've chosen to call '*Negen Zoete*' Kisses. It's clearly not *Neger Zoenen* – that would be offensive! …But it's enough like *Neger Zoenen* to appeal to all those those die-hard racists out there.

Maybe the blackface tradition will never change. But remember – the original Saint Nicholas came from Myra in Turkey. And if Sinterklaas' boat is supposed to come from Spain, then the dark-skinned Spaniards are Moors, from 'Morocco.' So even if you're offended by the blackface, just remember the biggest holiday of the Dutch calendar is actually being run by a Turkish guy and a bunch of Moroccans.

CHAPTER 11

Dutch Standards

It is tempting to make fun of Dutch '*gekke gewoontes*' (silly standards or habits). Yet they can make more sense than what you're used to.

QUESTION 1

When is a floor not a floor?

A – The thirteenth floor

B – The ground floor

C – The mezzanine

ANSWER = B

Most buildings count their floors from the good old number 1. But Dutch buildings start with the ground floor as 'Floor Zero.' For Americans, this is way too close to the term 'Ground Zero.' To make things clearer, a Dutch term for *floor* is *verdieping*. *Verdieping* means 'going deeper' – while you're actually going higher. No wonder MC Escher was Dutch.

QUESTION 2

What is the proper term for your relationship partner, when you've decided to do *samenwonen* (live together) instead of getting married?

A – Girlfriend

B – Wife

C – Baby Mama

ANSWER = NONE OF THE ABOVE

As of this writing, Dutch society still hasn't come up with a decent term for 'significant other.' I've met too many Dutch men my age, who still don't know how to refer to the female partner they've been living with for 10 years.

'This is my… girlfriend.'

'How long have you been dating?'

'We're not dating; we live together. She's like my wife.'

'How long have you been married?'

'We're not married … she's my partner.'

'So you're in business?'

'We're not in business. She's my… baby mama?'

Dutch people, you invented the term *samenwonen*. You really should figure out what to call the person you're spending your life with. Why not *samenwoman*?

QUESTION 3

How do Dutch people make a decision?

A – They flip a coin

B – They consult an astrological chart

C – They don't make a decision

Dutch Detour NO
Dutch detours be like: 'NO.'

Trick question! In the Netherlands, it's not about *making* a decision; it's called *taking* a decision. ...but *taking* it from where? Apparently, if you can't *make* up your mind, you need to *take* a decision from someone else. In the case of Dutch economic policy, they'll *take* their decision from, say, Germany.

QUESTION 4

How many of the following definitions could apply to the term *gas station*?

A – A place to put gasoline in your car

B – A place to put natural gas in your car

C – A place where the food will give you gas

The term 'gas station' is terribly unspecific. The Dutch have 'tank stations,' which is only confusing if you're driving a tank.

QUESTION 5

When does a Dutch person give you his cell number?

A – When he lives in a prison cell

B – When he is a monk

C – When he has been living in the United States

Americans have 'cell numbers' because they have 'cellular' phones. Dutch people will give you a 'mobile' number, because they have the much more sensibly named 'mobile phones.' It could be worse: the term for a German mobile phone is a 'Handy,' which only succeeds in making me giggle inappropriately.

The term c*ell number* should only have one meaning: you are in prison. Or perhaps you are a bee.

Of course, it can be confusing when you get caught in between cultures. If this happens, remember to just relax and 'go your gang.'

CHAPTER 12

Dutch Cuisine

On the international stage, cuisine can play a pivotal role. Compare the climate summits in 2009 and 2015.

In Copenhagen 2009, the Danish Environmental Minister had a simple strategy: lock the delegates in a room and don't let them out until they reach a deal. There was no deal. By contrast, in 2015, the French hosts stopped the whole summit to make sure everyone had enough to eat and drink. Even as the final negotiations were nearing completion, the French summit paused for coffee, croissants and chocolate. The resulting climate agreement was the most successful ever.

QUESTION 1
What did Dutch hosts serve European leaders at the 2016 event to kick off the European Presidency?

A – Cheese blocks and mustard
B – Herring and smoked eel
C – Coffee and mini muffins

ANSWER = A & C

For the first half of 2016, the Dutch played host to the EU Presidency. One of the stated policy goals was to avoid wasteful spending. Hence, the afternoon session featured coffee and mini muffins, and the evening session reportedly welcomed dignitaries with cheese blocks and mustard.

Rumor has it that there was also warm food. This probably means the Dutch delicacy known as 'bitter balls,' which is not a description of flavor as much as a way to describe how foreign dignitaries feel when presented with deep fried gravy. The deep-fried exterior of bitter balls will mask the scalding-hot inside, so that one can hardly take a bite without burning one's tongue within the first 30 seconds. After that, the Dutch hosts can serve any number of follow-ups from liverwurst to pickled onions and describe them as delicious. And the guests will have no choice but to take their word for it.

QUESTION 2
What does FEBO stand for?

A – *Frans & Eefje's Borrel Hapjes*
B – Ferdinand Bolstraat
C – Freshly Embalmed Bovine Offal

ANSWER = B

FEBO takes its name from its first-ever location on Ferdinand Bolstraat. Specifically, they took the FE from Ferdinand and the BO from Bolstraat. If they wanted to be more accurate, they could have just added two more letters and called their place 'FER BOL.' Because the inside of a *kroket* looks a lot like something a cat coughed up.

QUESTION 3
What is the favorite candy of the Dutch palette?
A – *Chocola*
B – *Drop*
C – Gummi

`ANSWER = B`

The favorite candy of the Netherlands is *drop*. It is called *drop* because it's the flavor most people usually drop on the floor at the movies. There are many different varieties of this black licorice flavor: hard, soft, sweet, and yes: salty. Some types of *drop* are so salty, they could be described as 'Industrial Accident Flavor.' They are specifically designed to make the human mouth never want to taste anything ever again.

QUESTION 4
What is the appropriate way to keep Dutch bread fresh?
A – Buy fresh bread for every meal
B – Buy fresh bread once a day
C – Buy fresh bread and keep it frozen/refrigerated

`ANSWER = B`

Dutch culture is so fanatic about fresh bread that it nearly impossible to *buy* fresh bread. The supermarkets do their best, building in little mini-bakeries in every store on every block. But even though the ovens are constantly churning, the fresh stuff is frequently sold out. Many Dutch abhor any preservatives with their food, including the preservative known as 'the refrigerator.'

KKK

'Your name is Kronenburg Group. What letters would
you like for your white van?' 'KKK, please!'

QUESTION 5

How can you tell when you've truly assimilated into Dutch culture?

A – When your mashed potato *stamppot* satisfies a Dutch family

B – When you really appreciate a cheese sandwich

C – When you spill chocolate sprinkles all over the floor and still scoop them and eat them, knowing chocolate sprinkles are indistinguishable from mouse poops

ANSWER = ALL OF THE ABOVE

My wife is Dutch, and my *stamppot* is good enough that she has asked me to make it more than once. As for option C, yes, I've done that. And as for option B, traditional Dutch sandwiches will be served with meat only or cheese only. I used to steal the cheese from one sandwich and combine it with the meat to make a more American sandwich. But there came a moment when I had an *oude kaas* (aged cheese) option. And I realized that – to combine it with meat or tomato would be a sin. When you can appreciate that the bread is truly fresh and the cheese is really old, then your palate understands the Dutch.

You may just want to choke it down with a tall glass of buttermilk. (Though that's a level of Dutchness I have not yet attained.)

CHAPTER 13

Dutch Group Behavior

Dutch people are famous for having a very open and tolerant society. The good news is: you can relax and be yourself. The bad news is: if you're not acting Dutch enough, they'll simply laugh in your face. Because they're also just being themselves.

QUESTION 1

Which is more important?

A – *Doe Normaal*, 'Do Normal'

B – *Doe Maar Gewoon*, 'Just act normal'

ANSWER = BOTH

For an open and tolerant society, there's a lot of emphasis on being *normal*. Perhaps it's the Calvinist history that requires Dutch people to '*doe normaal*.' The opposite of 'do normal' is bragging, or '*opscheppen*,' or 'piling it on.' Dutch culture is about equality. And if you try to act bigger than you are, Dutch people will quickly cut you down to size. To quote longtime Dutch resident

Pep Rosenfeld, 'The Dutch are very tolerant, as long as you do *normaal*.'

'*Doe maar gewoon*' also translates to 'just act normal.' But it has a follow-up: '*Doe maar gewoon: je bent al gek genoeg.*' Literally, 'Just be yourself. You're crazy enough as it is.' Yes, Dutch folks have a history of being tolerant. As such, they've seen it all before, and your version of 'crazy' is not so much shocking as 'probably annoying.' A building that looks like an enormous bathtub? That's just Dutch architecture. A man and a woman with their genitals pierced together? That's just a club night poster. A guy in a gold G-string dangling over your table while you're trying to order a drink? That's every Friday at Leidseplein. Just act normal.

QUESTION 2

You are in a queue at a public event and someone sneaks to the front. What do you do?

A – Look the other way. Pointing only makes it worse

B – Politely point out that there is a line

C – Pretend like you know the person and also sneak to the front

ANSWER = NONE OF THE ABOVE

The correct answer is:
Act like you've never heard of the concept of queuing and – if there are train doors involved – attempt to trample the slow and the weak.

Kut jas
For the Dutch speakers. Sometimes fashion
is *gewoon kut*.

QUESTION 3

You're at a Dutch comedy show and the performer onstage is very funny. How do you react? You:

A – Laugh out loud

B – Sit with your arms crossed and do not react at all

C – Yell out heckles at random moments to challenge the performer

ANSWER = B

For Dutch audiences, laughing out loud is considered rude and embarrassing, and it possibly causes cancer. Heckling is thankfully not for the Dutch, who leave that to the Brits and Irish. More important is to sit with your arms folded and offer nothing at all – until after the show. That's when Dutch audiences can more easily corner the performers and offer their highly valuable critique, such as 'I saw you onstage. You were funny, but not that funny.'

QUESTION 4

The Netherlands is a country that values the right to privacy. You are in public and someone is eating. What do you do?

A – Nod politely as you pass

B – Get something to eat yourself

C – Respect their privacy

ANSWER = NONE OF THE ABOVE

While most social interactions are dictated by the '*Doe normaal*' rule, according to which you act as if whatever is going on is perfectly normal, there is an exception when someone is eating in public. Then it is important to stare at them, point at them and say 'Eet smakelijk' (Bon appetit) as loudly as possible, until they choke on their food.

QUESTION 5

You are checking out at a Dutch supermarket, and you have too many groceries for one shopping bag. What should you do?

A – Ask the friendly staff to provide you with another bag and help you load your purchases

B – Ask the person behind you for a spare bag

C – Lower your head in shame and wait to be punished with eye daggers

ANSWER = C

You are expected to load all your purchases immediately, with no help from anyone else. You can buy another bag, but if you are not quick enough, the cashier will punish you by pulling in the *Beurt balkje*, otherwise known as 'The Game Over' bar. Your bread will be bumped, your eggs will be crushed, your bananas bruised. You must pointlessly load your items back into your shopping basket while avoiding eye contact and then do the Walk of Shame to the bag-loading area to wait in line again. By the end, hopefully the supermarket will have taught you a lesson not to spend too much money at their business.

CHAPTER 14

Dutch Stereotype: Cheap

Another stereotype about the Dutch is that they're cheap. This is not so much an international stereotype as it is one they have about themselves.

QUESTION 1

What is the meaning of 'Going Dutch?'

A – A date in which both parties pay half

B – A date in which someone tries to avoid paying what they owe

C – A date in which both parties take too much time negotiating over the bill

ANSWER = C

The traditional definition of a Dutch date is when both parties split the check. But a real Dutch date is when the bill is not simply split in half. Rather, it involves the phrases 'You had a more expensive starter than I did,' 'I only had beer, not wine,' and 'you owe me € 1.70.'

QUESTION 2
Where are Dutch people the least cheap?

A – Flevoland

B – Limburg

C – Noord Holland

ANSWER = B

In the part of the Netherlands known as 'below the rivers,' people are known as more generous (with the exception of one very guarded politician from Venlo). Many parts of Limburg in particular can't make up their mind if they're even *in* Netherlands – or Burgundian Belgium. My mother in-law lives on the border with Limburg, which is known for its fruit pie *vlaai*. Every time we go to visit, she'll serve a plate of *vlaai*, a cup of coffee, and then a cookie from the tin. More than once I've spilled the coffee, trying to balance this bounty of items. Wiping scalding hot coffee off my lap, I've sometimes wished for *less* generosity.

And let's not forget the generosity of the Dutch government for those who seek a tax haven. On the one hand the Dutch Finance Minister is known for saying that Greek people must pay their taxes. On the other hand, if Greek people were to register themselves as corporations in the Netherlands, they could get away with paying next to nothing.

QUESTION 3
Which term best describes Dutch cheapness?

A – Frugal

B – Humble

C – Stingy

As you may have read in *The Undutchables*, Dutch hosts will offer you cookies. But after you've made a selection, the cookie tin will close so quickly you might lose a finger. This is not to prevent you from stealing a second cookie. Rather, it is to keep the remaining cookies fresh. Other cultures just leave the cookies open (until they're all eaten). Coming from, say, America, it can be hard to understand quality over quantity. We just take one look and conclude 'cheap.'

But are the Dutch really cheap? Or are they more *zuinig*, which translates to somewhere between *frugal* and *stingy*. There's a reason so many Dutch businesses are into W2R (Waste to Resource). Case in point, they love TLA's (Three-Letter Acronyms).

Such as UCO (Used Cooking Oil): Dutch startup SkyNRG is recycling cooking oil to make jet fuel. Now, your next flight on KLM might be powered by LNF: Last Night's Fries.

Or CNG (Compressed Natural Gas): In Friesland, waste management company Omrin recycles and composts enough organic waste to have enough CNG to power their entire fleet of trucks – and have enough left over to add to the national gas grid. I asked the CEO 'Why isn't everyone doing this?' And he said 'Well, Groningen still has a lot of natural gas. I guess they like earthquakes.'

QUESTION 4
Which typical Dutch food is the most *zuinig*?

A – *Drop*
B – *Stroopwafels*
C – *Zoentjes*

Manwood

How can this not be a porno store?

Drop is not just made of anise flavor (your pronunciation of *anise* depends how much you like *drop*). *Drop* is made from gelatin. There's never been a better example of 'waste not, want not' than *drop*. At least not since the early Native Americans, who famously used all parts of the buffalo. Gelatin is made from cow hooves, cow bones, cow teeth, and 'Fallen animals.' According to the Benelux manufacturers of gelatin, fallen animals are the ones that are normally too sick to eat. It used to be that when they'd fall over and die, they'd have to be thrown away. But now – thanks to a new industrial process – when they drop, the Dutch make *drop*.

QUESTION 5
Which of the following public artworks typifies Dutch cheapness?

A   B   C

ANSWER = NONE OF THE ABOVE

The first sculpture is a series of metal tree trunks, located in a forest in Amsterdam. At some point, the city must have had a sack of money to plant some new trees, perhaps in an area that needed more trees. But no – instead, there was an artist who said 'I have an idea! Why not make people think about *dead* trees?' Less green, more death. If you can afford to think this way, you're not exactly cheap.

The second sculpture stands in front of an Amsterdam school. It's a sculpture of a man. How can you tell it's a man? Because of the huge, spiky steel erection. Necessary? No. Welcome? Probably not. But still funded with public money.

The third sculpture was commissioned for the opening of a public building in Amsterdam *Oud West*. Integrated into the façade of the building is a series of white ladders extending up and out and high above the street. At the top of the ladders is a life-size human figure with its arms stretched up to the heavens. And it's called 'How to Meet an Angel.' What is the public building that received such a sculpture? It's a mental health center for people with psychiatric problems.

If the Dutch can afford public art like this, then you can't call the Dutch cheap.

CHAPTER 15
Dutch Language

Speaking Dutch among Dutch people is rather like giving a toast while drunk. You know you're going to humiliate yourself and everyone watching, but you do it anyway.

QUESTION 1

Which is the correct meaning of the term *Hè hè*?

A – Pleasant weather

B – How hard was that!?

C – Oh, well

ANSWER = ALL OF THE ABOVE

There are many need-to-know definitions of the term '*hè hè*,' none of which are covered in your language textbook.

Definition A is when you walk outside after a week of rain, and suddenly the sun is shining. Here you are allowed to say '*hè hè*,' as in 'nice weather,' with the unspoken subtext '...*finally*.'

The second definition is used when someone finally succeeds at a task that should be easy. An example would be during penalty kicks for the Dutch national football team. (For those who don't follow football, or call it 'soccer,' penalty kicks work like this: a bunch of guys kick a ball around for two whole hours, but no one scores. That's when the referee takes the ball, puts it right in front of the net and says 'See if you can kick it in now.') When the Dutch national team finally scores during a penalty kick, the proper reaction is 'HÈ HÈ!?' (How hard was that?!)

And the third definition of '*hè hè*' is when the Dutch national team inevitably lose on penalty kicks and are again eliminated. Then the proper reaction is a series of nonsense syllables, followed by '*hè hè*': '*O, nee! Nee, joh! O, Sjonge jonge jonge! Nou, verdikkie… ahh, hè hè.*'

QUESTION 2
Which of the following is a Dutch word?
A – *Landje*
B – *Planeetje*
C – *Zonnetje*

ANSWER = ALL OF THE ABOVE

When in doubt, you can put a diminutive suffix on anything. Yes, you can look for a sizable house, but it's best to refer to it as a *huis-je*. Having acquired the little house, it is customary to acquire a tree: *boom-pje*. And a pet: *beest-je*.

What does it say about Dutch culture? Maybe it has something to do with growing up next to a big sibling like Germany. Some people call it an inferiority complex. Some say it's those Calvinist roots, demanding modesty in all things. But that's not quite it. While some cultures – say America's – like to 'Think Big,' the Dutch language forces you to celebrate scaling down. An entire country can be referred to as a *land-je*. And it's quite common to

 **Robbers**
Sinds 1920

Home | Contact | Nieuws | Vacatures

Over Robbers

Regionaal karakter

Onze medewerkers

Robbers
Trust them in your office or in your home.
Robbers.

hear Dutch people refer to the sun – *zon* – with a diminutive. The largest object in the solar system, and the Dutch call it *zonnetje*.

QUESTION 3

When you tell a fellow passenger in a train compartment you'd be happy to switch with them to ride facing backwards, you say '*Ik kan achterop rijden.*' What have you actually said?

A – I'll ride backwards
B – I'll ride on the back
C – I'll ride on your back

ANSWER = B

The word you were looking for is *achteruit*. But enjoy as everyone in the train compartment has a good laugh picturing you being dragged to your death behind the train.

QUESTION 4

When referring to a decision by the school board, you say '*De beslissing is ongesteld.*' What have you actually said?

A – The decision is mentally unstable.
B – The decision is being digested.
C – The decision is menstruating.

ANSWER = C

The word you were looking for is *uitgesteld*. Most Dutch people will know which word you were looking for. And they will still look at you with incomprehension and contempt.

QUESTION 5

When a group of orange-clad boys are playing football on the day of a big match for the Dutch World Cup team, you say '*Wat is je voorspel door vanavond?*' What have you actually said?

A – What is your prediction for tonight?

B – What is your foreplay for tonight?

C – What is your ball game tonight?

ANSWER = B

The word you were looking for is *voorspelling*. Instead, you're now the guy who goes up to kids on a playground and asks them about their sexual plans for later.

CHAPTER 16

Dutch Environment

The Netherlands is a river delta, and this country is so flat that even a city called 'Seven Mountains' (*Zevenbergen*) is one meter under sea level.

26% of this country wasn't originally land at all, and 50% could be flooded any minute. Personally, I feel like every day I survive in the Netherlands is a miracle.

QUESTION 1

Which phrase best describes the current Dutch attitude toward growth?

A – Full is Full

B – The polder model

C – 'On the eighth day, the Dutch made Holland'

ANSWER = A

Yes, Dutch history is all about draining water and creating land, or *polder*. You might think that – for a country that created much of its landmass using shovels and pumps – they'd be proud of their history of cooperation, known as 'The Polder Model.' But lately, the headlines indicate 'the Polder Model is dead.'

Perhaps its Dutch modesty that resists taking too much credit for their engineering successes. Look at Flevoland. Just 60 years ago, it was mostly underwater. Now it's an entire new province! The rest of world looked at the new Dutch map and said 'It's a miracle!' But ask any Dutch people about Flevoland, and the general response is 'Mwah, it's okay… It's not *gezellig*.'

The politician who says 'Full is full' more than anyone is Geert Wilders. In Flevoland, his PVV party gained a majority in the city council of the capital, Almere. This is especially ironic, because – if any city is not exactly full – it's Almere. And it's a bit odd to say 'Full is full' in a city whose land didn't exist 60 years ago. If you hear Dutch people say 'Full is full,' please remind them: 'You're Dutch! Just make more land.'

QUESTION 2
Which of the following is NOT a Dutch innovation?
A – Smog magnet
B – Solar bike path
C – Governmental climate action panel

ANSWER = C

There's no shortage of climate innovation in the Netherlands, but it's not coming from the Mark Rutte government. The smog magnet is an invention of Rotterdam designer and innovator Daan Roosegarde. It's being tested in China to remove smog particles from the air. The first-ever solar bike path is in Uitgeest. And as for the current Dutch government – they are doing so little to meet their own environmental goals that they were successfully sued by the Dutch group Urgenda, and that is a worldwide precedent.

So technically, yes the climate action panel helped create a Dutch innovation, but not in the way they intended.

QUESTION 3
Which of the following is NOT true?

A – 26% of the Netherlands is under sea level

B – Nederland is the 3rd biggest agricultural exporter in the world

C – 22% of the world's potatoes originate in Nederland

ANSWER = B

Actually tiny Nederland is the world's SECOND biggest agricultural exporter. Impossible as it may seem, a 2014 report from the University of Wageningen claims that Dutch exports of dairy, eggs, meat, flowers, fruit and vegetables are second only to the United States. Yes, European neighbors like France and Germany do produce a lot of food, but apparently they also enjoy eating it.

The Netherlands boasts 10,000 hectares of greenhouses. The Dutch are responsible for 22% of the world's exported potatoes. And according to Oxfam, the Netherlands is the world's number one country for plentiful, affordable food. How can this be?

According to *The Economist,* the Dutch secret is 'sustainable and intensive food production,' including innovations such as fermenting their hay. Fermented hay makes a big difference in cow poop. Mucking out the cowshed has been a Herculean task, ever since the Augean stables of Greek mythology. But by fermenting their hay, Dutch farms create liquid manure, which is removed by conveyor belt. It's apparently a game changer. The process of fermenting hay is so efficient that there's enough manure left over to

SP SENATOR TINY KOX

Tiny Kox (1953, Zeelst) acquired degrees in Eersel (1970) and Eindhoven (1973), and afterward received a law degree at the University of Tilburg (1975), where he has lived since 1973. From 1978 to 1982 he was active as the coordinator of the Tilburg legal-aid centre. In 1978 he became editor of the *Buurtkrant*, an activist housing bulletin published by the SP, of which he had become a member in 1975.

Tiny Kox
His name is *Martinus*. He could have chosen Martin. Or *Marty*. But no: *Tiny*.

create biogas to heat Dutch homes. Leave it to the inventors of the poop shelf to pioneer cow poop innovation.

QUESTION 4
Which of the following is a Dutch initiative?
A – Car-sharing incentives
B – Creating green space in cities
C – Importing foreign garbage for recycling

ANSWER = A & B

Yes, the Netherlands imports foreign garbage, but it's not for recycling. It's to keep up capacity in their big old incinerators. Meanwhile; yes, there are car-sharing incentives. And there's a trend for creating green spaces – largely by removing parking spaces. In fact, the largest incentive for car-sharing is that the parking spaces are disappearing.

QUESTION 5
Which of the following natural disasters resulted in help from the Dutch?
A – Hurricane Sandy
B – Hurricane Ivan
C – Hurricane Katrina

ANSWER = A & C

First came Hurricane Katrina in 2005, when Dutch expertise was called in to help prevent another disaster. A Dutch friend of mine works in Chicago, and he helped connect the Dutch engineering firm Royal Haskoning with the US Army Corps of Engineers. Up to that point, the US Army had been famous for its engineering of a shipping canal from the Mississippi to the Gulf of Mexico. It was the Dutch who pointed out that the canal also acted as an enormous storm funnel aimed directly at downtown New Orleans. Royal Haskoning are now helping build storm barriers to prevent another Hurricane Katrina. But they reportedly didn't want to make a big deal about it, because that would be bragging, aka *opscheppen*.

Next came Hurricane Sandy in New York, 2012. Again, America invited the Dutch to advise. Specifically, they asked Henk Ovink from the Dutch Water Management Ministry *Rijkswaterstaat*. I did an interview with Ovink, who reported that the Obama Administration was proud to show they'd learned from New Orleans. They'd built a breakwater so that any storm surge aimed at Manhattan would be deflected – towards New Jersey. Thinking holistically, Ovink asked 'How does New Jersey feel about that?' The New Yorkers reportedly replied, 'Forget about it!' Ovink still has some work to do.

CHAPTER 17
Dutch Politics

Especially if you're comparing to America, Dutch politics can seem like Alice *Through the Looking Glass*. Liberals are Conservative. Socialists are Republican, and the whole thing is mad as a hatter.

QUESTION 1
How many different political parties are there in a Dutch election?

A – Just enough
B – Not enough
C – Too many to comprehend

ANSWER = C

The Netherlands is a country with just 17 million people. And there are about 17 million different political parties. Every time there's an election, there are 10 parties you know, and another 10 you've never heard of. Some of which didn't even exist the last time around. Some of them are like the Unity Party in Almere, which consists of just two members. And of course one of them split off, and now they're fighting over who gets to keep the name

'Unity Party.' That's why there are so many political parties. The smaller the country, the more they like to disagree.

QUESTION 2
How are ruling coalitions formed?
A – Via the King
B – Direct voting
C – Electoral college

`ANSWER = A`

Nederland is a democracy. There are elections, and the most popular parties get to form a coalition, right? Wrong. That would be plain old democracy. In Nederland, there's democracy-PLUS!

After the voting, the head of state (the King) appoints an *informateur*. How is the *informateur* chosen? There's one, essential, qualification: neutrality. The *informateur* must be someone with no personal interest in the outcome of the cabinet. In the last cabinet, for example, one of the *informateurs* was Uri Rosenthal … who turned out to be a member of the cabinet. But surely, that was just a coincidence? The other *informateur* was Ivo Opstelten … who also got a place in the cabinet. In fact, he was Minister of Justice. At least he was, until he was caught funneling state funds to organized crime.

In the Netherlands, the government should sometimes be called an Ikea Cabinet: it looks good on paper, but it ends up a little crooked. Trust me, I'm from Chicago. I know crooked politics when I see them. So yes, the Netherlands is a democracy. But the key to Dutch democracy is one unelected guy, appointed by the King, who takes his favorite parties behind closed doors and *then* tells you what the *actual* coalition will be.

TITS
It's not vulgar; it's an acronym.
It stands for 'This is the Shit.'

QUESTION 3
According to most Dutch people, how are mayors appointed?
A – Elected by the city council
B – Appointed by the King
C – Appointed by the Cabinet
D – Direct election

ANSWER = EVERYTHING EXCEPT D

First, the King's Commissioner gets to pre-select a list of candidates. Then the candidates are reviewed by the city council's (secret) committee. Then they send their choice to the Cabinet's Minister of the Interior to be appointed. If you want to be entertained, ask any two Dutch people to explain this process and watch them argue, as they come nowhere near the right answer. The only thing of which everyone is certain: it's not D.

QUESTION 4
Who was voted politician of the year 2015?
A – Geert Wilders
B – Jesse Klaver
C – Alexander Pechtold

ANSWER = A

Geert Wilders was voted 'Politician of the Year 2015.' Although more accurate would be the year 1933.

QUESTION 5
How many members does Geert Wilders' *Partij Voor de Vrijheid* have?

A – Over 50

B – Over 1,000

C – Over 100,000

Uniquely, there's only one official member of *Partij Voor de Vrijheid* (which translates into 'Freedom Party'): Geert Wilders. Clearly this is a man with trust issues. In fact, Wilders has lived in permanent 24-hour protection since 2004. Some say he knows as much about freedom as Donald Trump knows about being humble.

Wilders campaigns against anti-social disrespect for Western values. As examples, you can look at Dutch headlines:

✔ The guy who head-butted someone at a bar and put him in the hospital

✔ Or the guy who committed sexual misconduct in the workplace

✔ Or the guy who beat up his girlfriend, while the girlfriend was pregnant

But actually, these headlines were about the PVV.

✔ Marcial Hernandez (head-butt)

✔ Eric Lucassen (sexual misconduct)

✔ Dion Graus (domestic abuse)

There's also the guy who had to step down because of financial impropriety. And the guy who got caught sending inappropriate tweets. And don't forget the guy who got drunk and went on a rampage in the Parliamentary press club. These are not just *supporters* of the PVV. They're elected members of Parliament for PVV.

With the kind of people Geert Wilders attracts, it's no wonder he doesn't want them in his party.

CHAPTER 18

Dutch Health Care

Some say socialized health care means long waiting lines for medical attention. But seeing a doctor in Nederland is not a problem. The problem is getting the doctor to *do* anything.

Most countries have doctors swear some version of the Hippocratic oath. In Nederland, there seems to be a different oath: 'As much as possible, I will tell my patients "Why don't you go home and get some rest?"'

QUESTION 1
In Dutch health care, what is the prevailing attitude toward drugs?
A – Recreational drugs are dangerous
B – Pharmaceutical drugs are expensive
C – Pharmaceutical drugs are dangerous

ANSWER = C

In the Netherlands, recreational drugs are largely regarded as a tourist thing. It's the pharmaceutical drugs that are considered truly dangerous. Many tourists assume all Dutch people are drug-dealing, drug-doing, baby-killing, grandpa-murdering homosexuals. Yet – if that was true – then you could get drugs from, say, the Dutch health care system, which is virtually impossible. According to *De Volkskrant:* 'Dutch doctors prescribe the least amount of antibiotics in Europe.'

In America, you can't get through a check-out line without being offered three different kinds of ibuprofen. In the Netherlands, if you try to buy ibuprofen, you get a small lecture: 'Are you aware what you're purchasing? Are you familiar with the workings of this drug? Have you taken into account the potential effects?!?' Yes. The effects of painkillers are to kill pain. But at the Dutch pharmacy they look at you like you might be a drug addict.

The Netherlands is a country where you can get smart drugs over the counter, no problem. And (with a weed pass), you can get hash over the counter, no problem. But if you want to get antibiotic medicine to heal your body, then it's: 'Get out of here, you sick, disgusting freak.'

QUESTION 2

If you ask your doctor for a local anesthetic during an operation, what response can you expect?

A – 'Don't worry. It will be quick'

B – 'I won't lie. This is going to hurt'

C – 'Pain is part of life'

ANSWER = ALL OF THE ABOVE

Dutch society deserves its reputation for being tolerant. This includes a rather high tolerance for pain – as anyone who's visited the Dutch health care system will know. In other countries, you

VD Water
If you want venereal disease, drink this.

may encounter the phrase 'This might hurt a bit,' and it hurts – a bit. Dutch health care professionals are more direct. They don't sugar-coat it. You will hear 'This is going to hurt.' And oh, it hurts.

Some countries believe a positive mental attitude can boost your health. Dutch research seems to have concluded: it's better to admit suffering is inevitable. If you ask for a painkiller, you will either be told 'Don't worry, it'll be quick.' Or you will even be teased for being weak. 'LIFE IS PAIN,' your doctor will say, not content to torture just your body, but also your naive worldview.

Traveling back to America, I'm confronted with the opposite extreme. Half the TV ads in the US are for some kind of pill. Over-the-counter painkillers are so abundant they may soon appear in boxes of cereal. But in the Netherlands, there are Dutch women who give birth with no anesthetic. My wife herself gave birth to our two children on our bed, with no epidural. My family back in the US still doesn't really believe me: 'But what kind of anesthetic did she use?' None. 'But what kind of painkiller?' Nothing but deep breathing. 'Are you sure you're safe over there?'

Yes. We're safe in the knowledge that life is pain, and overmedicating is for tourists.

QUESTION 3

Which of the following questions has appeared in the Dutch Assimilation Exam?

A – 'You've just had your fourth baby. How many more babies is it healthy to have?'

B – 'Your neighbors just placed a wooden stork in their front yard. Should you discuss where babies really come from?'

C – 'How long after a miscarriage does a woman resume menstruation?'

The Dutch author Rodaan Al Galidi reported seeing the question about miscarriage in his assimilation course, and it was corroborated by the examiners. I think anyone receiving this question on the exam should be able to submit a rebuttal question: 'What's this got to do with cultural assimilation?' If this question is on the assimilation exam, then somewhere there must be a med school gynecologists' exam asking, 'Who painted *The Nightwatch*?'

QUESTION 4

Which of the following is an acceptable way to show annoyance with another person?

A – 'Go get cholera'
B – 'Go get typhoid fever'
C – 'Go get cancer'

Dutch culture prides itself on its directness. In medicine, the same Dutch directness applies.

It starts with Dutch insults, which go medical right away. In English-speaking countries, one of the worst things you can say is 'F*** off,' which basically means 'go give yourself an orgasm,' which is comparatively quite polite.

Vondel Kids
Want a daycare free from inappropriate
physical contact? Try 'Fondle' Kids.

QUESTION 5
Which are Dutch terms used in childbirth?

A – Shame hair

B – Shame lips

C – Mother cookie

ANSWER = ALL OF THE ABOVE

No better way to remind you of your Calvinist past than terms like 'shame hair' and 'shame lips.' And the Dutch word for placenta is *moederkoek,* or 'mother cookie.' Perhaps, long ago, there was someone who was hungry for a post-birth snack.

As mentioned earlier, my wife gave birth to both our children on our bed, at home. But we didn't do it alone. We had very helpful midwives, who swooped in and made a whole production out of it. Particularly with our second child, the midwife's assistant was very earthy, touchy-feely. Immediately after the successful birth of our healthy boy, she conducted what I can only refer to as a shamanistic gore-fest. After cutting the umbilical cord, she stepped in with bravado and said 'But wait! There's more.' And she proceeded to do her version of the magician pulling handkerchiefs out of the sleeve. She pulled until she reached the placenta, but no one was there to catch it. The placenta hit the floor, and the blood sprayed all over the walls like a special effect in a horror movie.

The midwife's assistant then gingerly picked up the placenta and cradled it in her arms. It was like a little competition. The midwife was with our baby, saying, 'Ooh! Look, he's beautiful!' And next to her was the assistant, looking at the placenta, saying 'Ooh! Look at these beautiful textures! Did you know the placenta weighs as much as the baby? You made this. You did this! *Kijk, die mooie vliezen. Mooie moederkoek.* …Would you like to keep it?'

I stared at her for ten full seconds, before I volunteered, 'Wha?'

The assistant explained, '*De moederkoek*. Some people like to keep it.'

I wanted to know why. Are there really people who eat it? Is it a Dutch thing I don't know about? Maybe I don't want to know...

But my wife was looking at me over her shoulder, saying, 'I don't know. Maybe we'll want it. We can plant a tree with it...'

As I watched my newborn being neglected, it occurred to me, 'Let's not have this discussion now.' Sometimes, just give the people what they want. I told the assistant, 'Fine! Wrap it up. We'll take it.'

For months afterward, if you'd come to our house and drop in for dinner, we'd be ready. We'd just have to look in the freezer for fish sticks, pizza, or if you ever wanted to try some 'Mother Cookie,' we got it.

CHAPTER 19

Dutch Bikes Part 2

Since so many Dutch people ride a bicycle every day, the need for Dutch mandatory biking lessons is imperative. And since the Netherlands will never let that happen, here is second set of questions on biking etiquette.

QUESTION 1

What is the most annoying vehicle on the Dutch bike path?

A – Scooter

B – *Bakfiets*

C – Canta

`ANSWER = NONE OF THE ABOVE`

Yes, scooters are annoying, but they are in fact merely a litmus test to see how tolerant you are. In fact, the most annoying factor for me is the exhaust.

Clearly, there are worse things. Specifically, the things that block the path entirely. Sometimes, this can be the Double-Wide Chat-Rooms: people biking next to each other so engrossed in conversation they become unaware anyone might want to pass them.

Yes, the Netherlands is a crowded place, and you must be very spatially aware. …Unless you have a really good chat going on.

QUESTION 2

You are biking on a bike path marked 'no motor scooters,' when you encounter a motor scooter. What should you do?

A – Take no notice and wait for the police to take action

B – Roll your eyes and make a rude hand gesture

C – Make contact with the scooter and point to the 'No motor scooter' signs

ANSWER = B

Waiting for the police to take action is not an option, as that will never happen. Granted – with a simple traffic control – the police could rake in thousands of euros per week. With a traffic camera, they could make millions. But for now, they're happy just to spend money putting up the signs – and leaving it at that. The most common Dutch reaction is to roll one's eyes, make a rude gesture, and carry on. But if you should make contact with a scooter, and you're tempted to point to the 'no motor scooter' signs, you can also take the opportunity to whack them on the head and say 'You could have avoided that whack, if you'd worn a helmet, in the street.'

Woonshop Hardon

This is a housewares store run
by the family Hardon.

QUESTION 3

While biking, you come upon a sign saying 'Detour. Biking further will bring a € 50 penalty,' what do you do?

A – Ignore the sign. Bike further

B – Take a completely different route

C – Follow the detour

ANSWER = B

While some cyclists will ignore the sign (and rarely provide me the satisfaction of being stopped for a penalty), most cyclists will indeed deviate. Usually halfway through the detour I'll have come up with a totally new route too, and take that one. There's also the option of getting off your bike and walking through the road construction, but you run the risk of being run over – and laughed at – by the ones who ignore the sign.

It's hard not to encounter road construction in the Netherlands. Indeed, the Dutch term for 'Road Closed' is '*de straat is open*,' literally 'the street is open.' Clearly they're thinking from the street's perspective, and dammit, sometimes that street needs to breathe. Sometimes a street will be perfect for two weeks, and then it will be ripped up again two weeks later, for no apparent reason. Perhaps it's just to make work for the people called the Brick Flippers. You can watch as they pull the bricks up from one side of the road and replace them on the other side. This is the code of the Brick Flippers: 'Some bricks have been face down for two weeks! We must flip them to the other side. We have to be fair to both sides of the brick.'

QUESTION 4

While biking, you are flagged down by a pedestrian who demands you give him your bicycle. What should you do?

A – Bike away quickly

B – Call the police

C – Give him your bicycle

ANSWER = C

Since your bicycle is probably second-hand, it was probably stolen at some point, and it probably belonged to the pedestrian. Hand over the bike and tell yourself 'We had a good run.' If you're nice about it, he may let you ride on the back to wherever you're going.

QUESTION 5

A Dutch family of four is riding a bike with a papa who has placed a toddler on the front handlebars and a mama on the back, who is holding a baby. How will the police react?

A – Stop the family and instruct them on bike safety

B – Impound the bicycle and arrest the parents for child endangerment

C – Give them a fine for biking without lights

ANSWER = C

The Dutch family car is often a bike. There can be child seats on the back and a baby seat on the front handlebars. Do you need helmets? No. *Doe normaal.* Yes, there will sometimes be a windscreen for the baby seat. Because wind in the face is dangerous. But being hit by a truck? Nah. Police wouldn't stop the family for that. In fact, police wouldn't stop them if there was one kid on the front handlebars, one on the crossbar, two on the back rack, and another standing on top of them for a playdate.

The family of four mentioned above actually rode past my house once. Papa and toddler in front. Mama and baby on the back. No helmet, no harness. The mama held onto the papa with one arm and the baby with the other. And then she removed her arm from the papa so that these two life forms on the back were just balancing with no support. I thought 'This is like watching Cirque de Soleil.' The reason she moved her arm was so she could lift up her shirt and start breastfeeding on the back of the bike. Yes. That is how the Dutch roll.

Were they stopped by the police? No. But if they'd been riding at night without a light? That's a fine of € 50.

CHAPTER 20

Dutch Service

The term 'Dutch service' can be an oxymoron. In keeping with their non-hierarchical tradition, the rationale of Dutch service is often: 'Don't tell me what to do.' In the Netherlands they say 'The client is king (just not the boss).'

QUESTION 1

Which of the following is a Dutch waiter most likely to say?

A – 'You're right, your dish isn't cooked properly. I'll have the kitchen fix it'

B – 'Are you feeling cold? I can turn up the heat'

C – 'Thank you for holding the door open while I carry this tray'

ANSWER = NONE OF THE ABOVE

The correct answers would be:

A – 'No, I'm not taking your dish back to the kitchen. It's supposed to taste that way'

B – 'Why would I turn up the heat? I feel fine'

C – 'Holding the door open? What do you want from me? I'm not going to sleep with you'

QUESTION 2
How much tip is appropriate on a bill of € 77?

A – € 3

B – € 11.20

C – € 15

ANSWER = A

Think of Dutch tipping as the opposite of America. In the US, a tip edges upward from 15%. In the Netherlands, it edges up to the nearest round number. In the US, if you'd leave a $ 3 tip on a $ 77 check, they'd try to claw your eyes out. Conversely, in the Netherlands, if you'd pay € 92 euros for a € 77 bill, they'd look at you with a mix of confusion and contempt, like you're a pig trying to walk on two legs.

QUESTION 3
Which is the most *gezellig*?

A – A sociable place to hang out

B – A sociable place to work

C – A sociable place where workers hang out

ANSWER = C

On a sunny day in Amsterdam, it's lovely to see the café terraces fill up in an instant. Everyone is drinking and soaking up the sun. And there's probably someone smoking right next to you. And you can't actually get a drink. Because the one next to you with the cigarette is your waiter. Shouldn't they be serving drinks? 'Nah, we're just being *gezellig*.'

America is known as a land of rugged 'do-it-yourself' types. But in fact it's America where you're bombarded with 'Can I help you?' And in the Netherlands, when you want to order, you're on your own.

QUESTION 4

Which is the best example of Dutch hospitality?

A – Your neighbor invites you over, and you drop by with a gift

B – Your neighbor invites you over, and you wave at them through their front window

C – Your neighbor invites you over, so you make an appointment for sometime next month, and you try to make zero contact in the meantime

ANSWER = C

The very term 'Dutch hospitality' can get you into trouble. Even when people invite you over, it's by appointment only. Some Dutch people say, 'You simply must come visit!' But make sure you don't drop in unannounced. When you take up your neighbor's offer to drop by sometime, and they're about to have dinner, you may be invited in, but not to join them. Your host will just propose: 'While we're eating our dinner, you can sit in the other room and read a magazine. Smells good, huh?'

Yes, Dutch houses will display their street-level living rooms with the curtains wide open, as if it's an invitation. But don't be fooled. As soon as you ring the doorbell unannounced, the curtains will close, and the answer becomes 'We're not here!'

Worst Croissant
Dutch croissants are the worst.

QUESTION 5
What is the meaning of 'that is not possible?'

A – 'That is not possible'
B – 'That is not probable'
C – 'That is possible. I just don't feel like it'

ANSWER = C

The phrase 'that is not possible' is a favorite of desk workers, civil servants and especially the colleagues of those who have told you 'That is possible.' It is especially popular to anyone working on a *SERVICE TEAM*. Any time you hear the word *service* and *team* in Dutch, there's trouble.

But there is something about Dutch service that I've found to be integral to the Dutch experience. I remember the day I had this realization, when my wife and I had to get a new washing machine. The agent at the store said it would be no problem for his colleagues to remove the old machine before installing the new one, 'Because that is the job of the service team!'

Sure enough, the service team showed up, took one look, and said 'That is not possible.' My first instinct was to play the role of the self-righteous American: 'They said at store it should be possible! Now what about customer satisfaction? I mean, we are paying you!'

But then it struck me: 'Wait a minute – no. Maybe it's a whole different way of communicating.' I told my wife, 'Stand back, honey. I'm going to try to communicate with them.'

She said, 'Please don't try it in Dutch.'

I slumped myself down next to the delivery guys and said, 'Wow, this sucks for you. Big heavy washing machine. You guys have to lift it up and over. You have to lift heavy stuff all day. Don't you? You know, they said at the store that it would be possible. But I see now that it is not possible. So I guess, okay, you can go. Yeah. I guess I'll just have to do it myself. But I don't know, I might hurt my back. So I could call a neighbor or something. But what if he gets hurt, then I need insurance, which I don't have. So (sigh) I guess the best thing is just to take it back to the truck. You'll just have to return it …'

And they looked at each other, as if to say: 'Wow. That was really good complaining.' And then they said, 'Well, okay, we'll give it a try…' And sure enough: bam, it was done.

Complaining about life in Nederland really can help you assimilate into Nederland. It's that point when you say 'The service is terrible, the food is terrible, everything is so expensive and it's so damn small … I've had it! I hate this country! I'm leaving!' THAT'S when Dutch people will say 'Yes! Now you know how we feel. Come, live with us, you can stay.'

That's how to really communicate with Dutch people. And they don't teach you that at the *Inburgeringscursus.*

In Closing

Dutch culture has a lot of unique selling points in the world. Indeed – from dikes breaking to oil spilling to global warming – Dutch people have answers to a lot of the world's problems.

The problem is the rest of the world doesn't know about it. The rest of the world should give the Dutch more credit. But they can't – not as long the Dutch refuse to take any credit.

Nederland, take some credit! I get it, you're Dutch: being proud is not in your DNA. But you can learn.

Stop saying 'Full is full.' If the land gets too full, you'll just make more. You're Nederland!

Stop saying 'Our economy is in trouble …' You still have some of the lowest unemployment in Europe: You're Nederland!

Stop saying you're afraid Islam is taking over your culture. You're Nederland! In the most populous Muslim country in the world, half the population started out half-Dutch already.

And that's why I'm proud I learned how to be Dutch. I'm Dutch enough to be proud of the Dutch, and American enough to not care how loud I am about it.

The Author

Gregory Shapiro is known from Boom Chicago, Comedy Central and BNR Nieuwsradio. He is married to a Dutch woman, with whom he has two children. His YouTube channel includes *United States of Europe, Amsterdam Comedy Podcast* and *Planet Nederland,* nature documentaries about the Dutch.

Photo by Adrie Mouthaan